THERE IS BEAUTY IN THE BLEEDING

CHRISTINA HART

THERE IS BEAUTY IN THE BLEEDING

Copyright © 2017 by Christina Hart
All rights reserved.
Cover Art by Diana Gomes
Cover Design by Kat Savage

ISBN-13: 978-1979042901
ISBN-10: 197904290X

*For Pudge —
my little wolf.
I will love you for the rest of my life
and then some.*

THERE IS BEAUTY IN THE BLEEDING

THEY SAY

You shouldn't have come here alone.
I hear this place is haunted.
I hear the girl who lived here before
died a thousand small deaths before
she would ever put a dress on again.
I hear she watches the clock in the corner
and wonders how many years
went by today.
I hear they put two locks on the door
and boarded up the windows,
just to be safe, just to keep people away.
They say you can hear voices in here,
that shadows will pass by you
even during the day.
You shouldn't have come here alone.
I hear this place is haunted.
They say ghosts roam these halls
and she lets them.
They say these walls aren't high enough
to keep the bad away.
They say beautiful things can be ugly, too.
They say beautiful things can deceive you.
They say if you ask her, she'll tell you
it's true.
They say a home can still be hell.
They say secrets keep you sick.
They say if you look like love

she will try to keep you.
They say others have left
sick
like her.
They say her voice echoes down their halls.
They say she got in their head.
You shouldn't have come here alone.
I hear this place is haunted.
I hear she'll tell you to leave
before you get too close.
I hear she'll tell you to run,
to never look back,
to never come this way again.
I hear it hurts her.
I hear it would hurt you, too.
You shouldn't have come here alone.
I hear this place is haunted.

THE SLAUGHTER IS GORGEOUS

Beginnings are beautiful—
the potential, the hope,
the realization that you can still **feel.**
But the endings
are where the magic happens.
The world crashing down around you
as you reassemble all the parts
that make you.
The slaughter, if you think about it,
it's gorgeous.

CHRISTINA HART

YOU WANTED ME TO WRITE ABOUT YOU

You wanted me to write about you
and I told you that was something
I couldn't do.
I told you I wasn't the kind to
write happy things.
You wanted to be the epicenter
of my tiny universe and for seven months,
you were. You ruled every little planet
that circled around me, and I let you.
There is something almost endearing
about possessive qualities, you see.
Something sick in me told me
that was real love, to be loved that much
they wanted you all to themselves.
You wanted me to write about you
and nothing else.
And the stubborn in me
just wouldn't fully give in so
I wrote nothing. I wrote nothing
until I no longer could so I wrote you
a goodbye you might never understand.
You wanted me to write about you and
I told you you wouldn't like it if I did.
You wanted me to write about you
and now I have.

THERE IS BEAUTY IN THE BLEEDING

AND NOW I HAVE

You wanted me to say things
I couldn't.
Not because I didn't feel them
but because I didn't feel them yet.
You were a pusher and I am the type
that pushes back.
And we both pushed
so far
and so hard
that I can't even see
where we started.
By the end, I didn't know
where the grass ended
and where the mud began.
I didn't know whether we were
sinking or swimming,
building or shrinking.
And I catch myself
wishing you were here,
but I am sick
of burning myself
on all the "what ifs"
on the way out.

THE GOOD TIMES ARE CUTTING ME

I put times spent with you
in boxes for storage and
packed them away in some
dingy dark corner in my mind
and for some reason, I just can't
allow them to collect dust.
I take them out and unpack them
so often even though every single time
that I do, I'm left sitting here
alone
with blood all over my hands.

THERE IS BEAUTY IN THE BLEEDING

LET THEM CUT YOU, TOO

There will be days when you completely
f a l l   a p a r t
and that's okay.
There will be days where your ribs
feel like blades.
Let them cut you.
There is beauty in the bleeding.
There is hope in the healing.

YOU WILL DIE FIRST

I don't expect you to stay.
Just give me something
I can write about later,
when you leave.
When you take that part of me
I didn't know I was offering.
I promise I will squeeze
the juice out of every memory
until there's nothing left of you.

THERE IS BEAUTY IN THE BLEEDING

AND I WILL WATCH

We were too busy
to find new flames.
We were still
watching everything burn
from our past loves.

CHRISTINA HART

SOMETIMES I WONDER

Sometimes I wonder if they can
still smell me on their sheets or
if they just think of me whenever
loneliness wraps her hand
around their throats.
Maybe they feel me in the squeeze,
maybe they remember me
in the choke.
Or maybe I am their safe word,
because the ones who leave,
they always come back.
And they are never whole.
And neither am I.

WHO I AM

I am playing hide-and-seek
with the person
I used to be and
the person I could be and
I cannot find either of them
anywhere.

# LET ME TELL YOU

Let me tell you about regret
and the way it sneaks up on you
in the middle of the night and
crawls into bed with you.
Let me tell you about loss and
the way it burrows into your bones
and becomes a part of you.
Let me tell you about abuse
and control and how you can
mistake it for love.
Let me tell you about trying to forget.
Trying to forget.
Trying to forget.
And failing.

THERE IS BEAUTY IN THE BLEEDING

ABOUT NOT BREAKING

They tried so hard to break me,
but they didn't try hard enough.

CHRISTINA HART

YOU TOOK MY HEART

When you left
you tore my heart out
with your hands and
carried it away
between your teeth.
But it was beating
just for you.
And all I could think
was how god damn good
it looked on you.

THERE IS BEAUTY IN THE BLEEDING

KEEP IT, KEEP IT ALL

I had to kill
certain parts of me
that only live now
in the memory
of you.

CHRISTINA HART

OLD HOLLYWOOD

I watched you in slow-motion
at first, then you moved
gracefully and rapidly,
in and out of scenes meant
for an old Hollywood movie,
until you slowly and quietly
faded out,
taking all the
romance and glamour
with you.

THERE IS BEAUTY IN THE BLEEDING

THAT BITCH

Regret comes often,
pounding on my walls,
waking me up at all hours
of the strange space
between night and morning
with a punch to the gut
and just once
I wish that bitch
would bring flowers or
an apology of her own.

CHRISTINA HART

I WONDER

We broke up on the 13th
and by the 14th
I would wonder if
I made a mistake.
By Halloween I would wonder
what you were dressing up as and
by Christmas I would wonder what
I would have gotten you as a gift.
By New Year's Eve I would wonder
who you were kissing and if
it should have been me.
By your birthday I would wonder
if you ever still thought of me at all
and by my birthday I would wonder
if you would have surprised me with
something. I would wonder if you
had become the **you** I always knew
you could be and if another girl
was lucky enough to call that guy hers.
I would wonder
why I still look at you as
mine
and I would wonder
if you still look at me as
yours.

THERE IS BEAUTY IN THE BLEEDING

ABOUT THE PAST

Living in the past
takes up a lot of time.
Sometimes it will even
take your future
if you let it.

CHRISTINA HART

SPEAKING OF REGRET

When the hurricane hit
we lost power for two weeks but
I had candles and I had you.
I think about the night I pulled out
my acoustic Washburn guitar and
you played motorcycle drive-by and
sang to me and it was the sweetest
sound I'd ever heard.
Since I left you,
the sun goes down in my eyes
every fucking day
and this aching in my chest
when I think of you
is enough to bring me to my knees.
I murdered us, I know.
I deserve every ounce of regret
in my coffee each morning.
And I'm sorry.
I miss you.

THERE IS BEAUTY IN THE BLEEDING

IT'S A VICIOUS RECYCLE

I'll just keep
collecting scraps
of trash
from my head
and my heart
until it all
stops
stinking.

PICKING PEOPLE APART

I'm sorry that I pick people apart,
dissecting them into fragments
of things I like and
things I don't like,
because when I try to
piece
them
back
together,
they're never the person
I thought they were, or the person
they might have been.
Either way, it's never enough.

LIKE WILTING PETALS

I find wilting petals
the prettiest.
They have a certain spirit
to them, wanting to
crumble and break,
yet fighting to stay alive,
and I never know if
I should water them
or just let them die.

CHRISTINA HART

I COULD NEVER LOVE THEM

One day
they'll carve names
in the stone of my heart
and ask me why
I wouldn't receive them.
I will tell them the truth—
I could never love them
the way they deserved.

THERE IS BEAUTY IN THE BLEEDING

BUT IT WAS CUTE THAT I TRIED

Acute delirium
was never
as cute
as it was
with you.

CHRISTINA HART

DROWNING IN SOMEONE

I have always been good
at saying the wrong things,
and using your name
like a lifeboat, as a
just-in-case I don't feel like
drowning in someone else
who might hurt me
the way you did.
I've gotten used to the
way *empty* feels,
used to the way
that when this pen dries up
I just dip it into
memories of you.
But the memories are not you.
I am learning a new language.
I am swirling in colors
that no longer look good on you.

THIS IS NOT LOVE

Maybe you thought
you were doing me a favor
when you tried to love me
the only way you knew how.
And I would tell you
this isn't love,
but I can't speak
with all the daisies
you stuck in my throat.

CHRISTINA HART

NEVER A CLEAN BREAK

I have broken hearts and
I have broken the law and
I have broken plates and
I have broken parts of myself
and I have taken others and
tried to put them back together.
It is so much
e a s i e r
to break things
than it is
to fix them.

REMEMBER?

I've been getting by on stale hope
and promises I swore you'd keep.
I've been driving for hours and
I can't see a thing
other than your face,
smiling, next to her.
I've been listening to Glycerine
on repeat to
try to remember the you
that I thought was honest.
You used to sing it to me,
remember?
But you sing it to her now,
don't you?
And I know her name.
I knew it back when you swore
she was nothing. And I swore
I believed you. And I swore you were
the one for me.
But the one for me wouldn't do this to me.
And this is goodbye.
And the next man won't suffer because
of you and I won't suffer because of you
and all the shit you never meant.

CHRISTINA HART

I HATE YOU, I MISS YOU

A painting in vengeance,
a palette of blacks and blues.
A subtle shade of pink for the lips
I won't allow myself to ever kiss again.
A doormat of too many footsteps.
A door opened and closed
too many times.
A goodbye note smeared
with no kiss.
An "I miss you" hanging
from my lips.
I'd paint you something,
but this particular blue
is too soft for that.

THERE IS BEAUTY IN THE BLEEDING

BUT I WILL LIVE ON

I hear the familiar drip
in the space heater and know
I am home.
These bones of mine
are used to the cold.
It is how I've come to
appreciate any warmth at all.
Some may call it unfortunate,
I call it the opposite.
No, I feel bad for those
who have no idea what it
means to suffer,
because have you lived
until you have lived on?

CHRISTINA HART

WRECKAGE

When everything feels harder
than it once was,
I need you to remind me
of the soft places within me.
When I am standing
amidst the wreckage,
remind me to dance.

SHOULD BE KEEPING YOU WARM

The leaves are falling again,
reminding me that another season
has passed without you.
I put a sweater on today but it is
just a not-so-cozy reminder
of the flesh and bones
that I am missing.
It should be you keeping me warm.

CHRISTINA HART

I AM NOT A DIRT ROAD

It was too late for us
when I realized
he was just a country song.
One I'd never heard,
one that never played for me,
and one I'd probably
never listen to anyway.

THERE IS BEAUTY IN THE BLEEDING

I AM THE TOWN

I am the flat tire in that
old Chevy in your backyard
you keep meaning to fix.
I am the alarm clock
going off in the morning
when you hit snooze and
say "five more minutes".
I am that novel you
never finished.
I am the milk you
forgot to drink
before it all went sour.
You ran out of time and
I am rotten now.
It feels good
to pour myself out.

CHRISTINA HART

DYING IN MELODIES

And he wrote a beautiful song
about a beautiful girl he loved
and I thought,
I've been falling in love
with the wrong musicians.
None of them made me
live forever in their chorus.
I've been dying in all the melodies
they forgot to write down.

THERE IS BEAUTY IN THE BLEEDING

IT WILL COME FOR YOU, TOO

It came too quickly,
sudden and sad
like a Monday morning,
this force of forgetting you.
But you,
you will always be my Sunday.
Long and quiet,
but not quite long enough.
Never long enough.
Never as long as my
longing for **y o u.**

CHRISTINA HART

TELL ME

Tell me where it hurts, little girl.
Tell me how you still remember
the bad men who made you
think your parts belonged to them.
Tell me when their waves
met your shore and you wanted
to forget your own name.
Tell me when your flower
stopped blooming.
Tell me when **trust**
became just a word.

THERE IS BEAUTY IN THE BLEEDING

ONE TRUTH

There is always an escape.
There is never an escape.

CHRISTINA HART

I WILL TELL YOU

I've seen warning signs and
duct taped clear skies over them
for the sake of feeling something like
love.
I've seen stability and invented stage six
hurricanes and inserted heavy winds
for the sake of feeling something like
passion.
I guess I've always wanted to see
how turbulent things could get
before everything explodes.
And when the winds chase you,
just know it only happens
to those I want to stay.

WHAT LOVE ISN'T

I am still learning about love
and what it should be.
I am still learning about love
and what it isn't.

CHRISTINA HART

A PRETTY LIE

My thighs are still sore
from your body
pressing into mine and
it's been two days
since I left my temporary place
in your bed and
moved into that space
in my head where I can
still hear you saying
you are different.
A lie dressed up in pretty words
is still a lie
and this time,
I won't forgive you.

A LITTLE WILD

I was wild once.
Free.
Unchained to anything
I didn't choose to attach myself to.
I feel it's only proper
to reintroduce myself.
You should run now.
Fear is behind me,
and he's a hell of a lot scarier
than you are.

CHRISTINA HART

WHEN NIGHT FALLS

And sometimes,
not all the time,
I am overcome by how much
I fucking miss you and
it's a quick right hook
I never saw coming and my
nose won't stop bleeding and
I don't cry, won't cry,
until I'm crying out for
someone to bring you back to me.
It's okay, I'll be all right
in the morning.
Until night falls.
Until I give in and fall
right along with it.

I WAKE UP

It is a strange thing,
waking up,
realizing you trust no one,
not even yourself.
It is stranger to realize
you feel this way because of
someone you thought you could trust.
And when they ask me
what happened,
when they ask me why,
I will sketch them
a picture of you and
they still won't understand.
And they don't need to.
I don't need them to understand.
I need them to go away.

ANGELS

He kept me on my feet,
in a place that was
a few shades lighter than hell.
But that didn't make it
burn any less.
And it didn't stop the angels
from going mad.

THERE IS BEAUTY IN THE BLEEDING

DISGUISED IN PRETTY DRESSES

People say that peace
will come one day
and I just wonder
if I'll think it's chaos
disguised in a pretty dress.

CHRISTINA HART

LET'S GO BACK TO DECEMBER

Hey you.
Yeah, you.
Let's go back to December.
Before the abandoned building,
because it was never abandoned.
You were never abandoned.
Let's go back to the nights
we spent high out of our minds
looking at the stars.
And the joke is on me
because you're up there now.
You never did realize how
captivating your smile was,
how your soft eyes were
too warm for this earth.
For years you have been playing
Lost & Found
but you were never lost to me.
And when I see you again
I will say the same six words to you
that I would have said before
December hit with the assault.
"I have been looking for you."
Did you miss me?
I've missed you, too.

BEFORE I NEEDED TO BE A HERO

In a better world,
I would have saved you.
In a perfect world,
you wouldn't have
needed saving
at all.

CHRISTINA HART

THE STRANGE WAY

I don't know if he notices
the strange way
my heart beats
when he fills the space
around me.
It's a drum roll—
waiting for him to
come closer and fill
the empty space within me.
And a sad melody—
knowing he never can.

I DESERVE THIS

Maybe one day
I will find a pair of arms
to wrap around me
as I deserve.
And that's exactly
what I'm afraid of.

CHRISTINA HART

TEACH ME HOW TO LOVE

Technology killed romance.
Stuffed it into a text message
that never sent and
smashed the flip phone.
Buried it in the backyard
with the time capsule
you hid when you were 10.
OK Cupid, grab your shovel
and start digging.
Teach us how to love again,
the old-fashioned way.
The right way.

THERE IS BEAUTY IN THE BLEEDING

I WILL TEACH YOU HOW TO PRETEND

If you need me,
I'll be wasting time on temptation,
handing out parts of me
like candy hearts on the
saddest Valentine's Day
you have ever known.
Tomorrow I will forget them
and turn up the volume
on the TV and pretend
I do not miss you.

Leave

I collect my earrings
off the stoop by the mailbox
and remind myself
he isn't worth it.
And they never are, are they?
If I paid attention
I'd notice that their bags
are packed before they
even say hello.
But I don't,
because I'm already mapping out
escape routes with a sharpie
and a tired heart and a one-way
ticket for the first one
who leaves
before they are left.

THERE IS BEAUTY IN THE BLEEDING

BEFORE YOU ARE LEFT

That's the problem
with giving someone
your body.
Sometimes
you never get it back.

CHRISTINA HART

LIFE WITHOUT YOU

Losing you
feels a lot like
counting backwards
from 10.
And I never know
where I'll wake up
on the other side
of this life
without you.

I WILL SAY IT IS EASY

I'm just going to lie
and tell you
starting over was easy.
I will say strong legs
are built from running and
hearts are hardened from hurting.
I will say you will be the same
as you were
before this changed you.
I will lie to you.
And you will like it.

CHRISTINA HART

I CAN LIE, TOO

I do not remember your hands
or the way you smiled when you were tired.
I do not remember the way your eyes
would crinkle when you just wanted
to sleep after a long day of loving me.
And when they ask me how I am,
I will say I'm fine.
And when they ask me if I miss you,
I will say no.
I can lie, too.
I learned from the best.

THERE IS BEAUTY IN THE BLEEDING

ABOUT US, ABOUT YOU

I had a dream of you.
And in it,
you loved me too.

WE GET UP

And the saints all watched in horror
as we did the ungodliest of things,
to ourselves, to each other,
as we loved in the most merciless ways,
as we fought this life with chipped nails
and dirty hair and unkempt personalities
and fractured hearts that somehow
kept beating, even after we beat
ourselves to near death and then some.
But every time, every day, we get up and
brush ourselves off and roll up our sleeves
and pretend we're all
just
fucking
fine.

THERE IS BEAUTY IN THE BLEEDING

TO WHAT WE KNOW

I read a line by Scott Laudati
that said there's a different kind of art
to wake up for. A family, children, and a
spouse. But I have no one to cook breakfast
for, no one to surprise with their favorite
ice cream, and unlike City and Colour,
I'm not coming home, because there's no
home like that to go to.
No home like that I know.
There's a 70-year-old woman I work with,
a friend, she pulled her tooth out the other
day with a pair of pliers. Peroxide played a
role. This is the shit I know. The art
I wake up to. And I might not have kids, or
a husband, but I have cigarettes and duct
tape and somewhere in there,
there's fucking love.

THESE BURNT CHILDREN

God forgive me,
I have sinned,
and I'm sure I'll sin again.
I may never understand
why the things
that are bad for me
give me so much pleasure.
I secretly enjoy the
aftertaste
of a beautiful let-down.
The hell keeps me warm.
I love the bittersweet chaos
in the aftermath
of my choices.
And I can't stop now,
there are too many mistakes left
to be made in my name.
These burnt children,
born and left in the rubble,
they are what I will leave behind.

THERE IS BEAUTY IN THE BLEEDING

THEY WILL NEVER UNDERSTAND

And then the words
didn't come
because all I heard
was you.
It was a silent film
played in color
and noise
and they would
never understand.

CHRISTINA HART

I DON'T KNOW WHAT I LIKE MORE, THE STARS, OR

I hate the distance
I tend to create.
I was never the type
to reach for the stars.
Instead, I was building walls
between us.
From my view,
I can't even see the stars anymore.
I can only remember
what they looked like
before I blocked them all out.

THERE IS BEAUTY IN THE BLEEDING

THE SCARS

In certain lights,
the scars you left me with
look kind of cute,
reminding me
that there is a possibility
I might never heal,
and I may never want to.

IF I'M BEING HONEST

He loves me
and ruins me
all at once
and honestly
I don't know
which I like more.

I WAS BORN THIS WAY

In love,
I am a god damn
kamikaze pilot.

In life,
I refuse to go down
with the plane.

OUR LOVE WAS

When I think about love
I think about you
and all the ways you moved me
but didn't at the same time.
You had flaws and so did I,
but damn it, you changed me
in ways no one else has
and now, I can't be with someone
who doesn't, because if
they don't inspire you to
be a better person,
what the fuck is the point?

ON FIRE

It's not about the spark,
it's about the **fire.**
It's your hands in my hair
never growing tired of the knots.
It's your snore and me
never getting tired of it.
It's seven blocks in the rain
in heels and no umbrella
and the only shelter being
your jacket and your laughter.
It's your cynicism and my sarcasm.
Your blue to my black.
Your gold to my white.
Your jazz to my punk.
Your
you
to my
me.
Every beautiful thing in you
that compliments all the ugly
in me.

CHRISTINA HART

TRYING TO GET BY

At the end of the day,
we were all just people,
trying to live,
trying to get by on
the little amount of money
we had and our love
for whatever we had love for,
if we even had any love left.
We grew up on the notion
that life wasn't fair,
but my god,
what an understatement
that was.
Life wasn't only unfair,
it was a kick in the groin
with a promise of hope.

THERE IS BEAUTY IN THE BLEEDING

ON SADNESS

There's a terrible sadness in me
and I don't know if it's personal
or just part of being human.

I'VE GOTTEN GOOD

He had a thing for names
and I wondered how he felt
about mine.
I wondered if he ever noticed
the way my insides shake
when he's around.
It's so loud.
It's all so loud.
But I've gotten good
at keeping the thunder quiet.
I've mastered the art
of concealing my hunger,
even when my ribs are showing.
I just wear loose clothing and
pretend that I am fine.
I double up my socks
to try to make up
for the lack of warmth
that should be from his arms.
And I carry on,
because it's the only thing
I can do.

THERE IS BEAUTY IN THE BLEEDING

AT HOLDING IT TOGETHER

No one wants to
hold these hands.
I don't blame them,
I can hardly hold them
t o g e t h e r.

CHRISTINA HART

IT'S JUST US

I was never big on red
but I was always sold on you.
I painted those Converse
black and sharpie'd your name
on the palm of my hand.
Those old chucks walked
for miles and months
to try to reach you.
But the black faded back to red
and you, you faded back to her.
And I was sixteen with the hope
that our favorite band would save us
but they didn't, they never could.
2006 was full of you,
my red converse and you.

THERE IS BEAUTY IN THE BLEEDING

IN THIS GRAVEYARD

The graveyard
is no place
for lovers
who aren't us.

LIFE IS ART

Sometimes life was reruns of Happy Days
and just enough toothpaste.
Sometimes it was chain-smoking
and getting drunk on Wednesdays.
Sometimes it was a dead battery
and no one around to give you a jump.
Sometimes it was sleeping in
until noon and still tired and restless.
Sometimes it was a 5AM wake-up call
and 10 minutes to get ready.
Sometimes it was music that played
over and over in your head.
Sometimes it was your favorite scent.
Sometimes it was your lover's smile.
Sometimes it was losing the very thing
or person that made you happy.
Sometimes it was hell.
But always, always, it was art.

THERE IS BEAUTY IN THE BLEEDING

ON THE EDGE OF SANITY

I believe in
pushing yourself
to the edge of sanity,
and then jumping.

I CAN DREAM

Another summer gone
with no trips to the beach,
but I can dream,
I can always dream.
I imagine lying on the warm sand
with a body full of life and love
next to me.
Put a little more sunscreen
on my shoulder.
Hand me my book
while you doze off.
I'll watch you fall asleep,
keep an eye on your chest,
the slow up and down,
to make sure you're still breathing,
to make sure your heart
is still beating for me.
And I'll forget about my book
because now is about you.
It's always about you.

THERE IS BEAUTY IN THE BLEEDING

A LITTLE DREAM

The bags under my eyes
are filled with dreams
that haven't come true yet.

CHRISTINA HART

STUCK SOMEWHERE

Right now I'm stuck somewhere
between what if,
what might,
what could have,
and what never will
and all I want to know
is what actually is.

THERE IS BEAUTY IN THE BLEEDING

TRYING TO BE OKAY

And maybe life isn't about
growing up or moving on,
maybe it's about being who we are
and where we are
and being completely okay with it.

CHRISTINA HART

VIOLENCE AT ITS FINEST

For years I thought love
sounded like screams
and chairs hitting the wall
and I thought love
looked like black eyes
and bloody lips and
I knew love was violence
at its finest and most forgivable.
For years I have been relearning
what love is and
what it should look like.
For years I have been waiting
for someone to show me.

THERE IS BEAUTY IN THE BLEEDING

DOES IT SCARE YOU?

Mornings are a time
for reflecting
on what terrorizes you
in the night.

YOUR BODY IS BEAUTIFUL

I wish they'd ask more.
I wish they'd tell more
on a first date.
Forget where I work.
Forget how much you make.
I'm more interested in knowing
if you're the type
to take my hands
when I cover myself.
I want to know if
you will say
"Don't hide your body,
it's beautiful."

THERE IS BEAUTY IN THE BLEEDING

BUT YOUR GUTS ARE PRETTIER

I try not to
spill my guts
because
every
time
I do,
there's a
huge
fucking
mess
to clean up.

CHRISTINA HART

BUILT TO PLEASE

He told them I was easy.
Easy, as if it wasn't hard
for me to trust him.
Easy, as if my clothes
slipped off at the snap
of his fingers.
Easy, like I was built to please.
Easy, as if that word
wouldn't cut me down.
Easy it was for him.
It was as easy for him as
it is hard for me
to say what I mean:
I just don't want to be hurt anymore,
and I don't want to hurt anyone else
in trying to avoid that.

BUILT TO REGRET

I take trash bags
filled with regrets
out to the curb,
daily,
but no one ever
picks them up.

THEY WORSHIP US

He can't tell me what it feels like
when he says I'm beautiful
and then shrugs me away.
He doesn't know how this body
feels like a tomb
and how these kisses
have turned into carnage
but he is lost in between my legs,
every sister, every daughter,
and they worship us,
just not in the way
we need them to.

THERE IS BEAUTY IN THE BLEEDING

THEY TRY TO DESTROY US

In the end,
we're left
with the pieces
no one could break.

/ CHOOSE TO LISTEN

I love when it rains,
when it seems like
the sky has had enough
of keeping it all in
and finally explodes
with a torrential downpour
of all the shit
it's been meaning to tell us
but didn't have the courage to
until right now.
And me?
I choose to listen.

THERE IS BEAUTY IN THE BLEEDING

I CHOOSE TO IGNORE THEM

And then I realized
the problem wasn't
all the things
they said about me,
the problem was
that I believed them.

YOU ARE A FUNERAL

You left me with
nothing
and
everything
wrapped up in
a pretty package
for no one to open.
You are
Christmas morning
at a funeral.
I am the aftermath.

BUT DARLING, I DIED YEARS AGO

Save your energy
for the next one, darling.
I beat you all to it.
There's nothing left
to destroy here.
I self-destructed years ago.

I TOLD YOU

When I think about you
I think about Main Street
and cold feet and sobriety
and how life itself
scared the hell out of you
and so did I
and our love was so new,
so strong, so rare,
and you told me
you'd never love anything
more than heroin
but I thought
I could prove you wrong
because I wanted so badly
to believe we could make it.
Sometimes I hear your voice
whispering "I told you so"
when I'm lying alone in bed.

NOT TO SCREAM

Sometimes you just
have to bite the bullet
and try not to scream.

CHRISTINA HART

I WANT TEN SHOTS OF LOVE

There was no trick
to falling in love.
All it required was
an inhuman taste
for a grand buildup
and subsequent
disappointment.
It was never a secret,
we just didn't
want to admit it.

THERE IS BEAUTY IN THE BLEEDING

AND KEEP THEM COMING

Sometimes you just
have to chase the regret
with a shot and
pretend you
meant to do that.

WILD THINGS

Dunkin Donuts coffee and
a midnight meet.
You smiled and I felt
that wild thing in my chest
start to move,
start to constrict.
We told secrets in parked cars
and it smelled like love.
Tonight I will wash the
death off my hands
and think of you.

THERE IS BEAUTY IN THE BLEEDING

IM ONE OF THOSE, TOO

I stopped being
afraid of the
monsters
under my bed
when I realized
I was one, too.

CHRISTINA HART

USED AIR

I've been fucked with,
stomped on, used,
toyed with, and left to rot,
and I'm not sure
I know exactly what love is
but I know what it's not.
Hell, I'm not even sure
the air I breathe is mine,
it very well may be
pieces of lovers left behind,
reminding me every so often
to gasp for air and inhale,
giving me a little pat on the back
and reminding me not to die just yet,
so I don't. I keep going,
realizing some things in me
are a little broken,
a little unbreakable,
or a clusterfuck of both.

THERE IS BEAUTY IN THE BLEEDING

BURNT HEART

Heart
is that stubborn
part of you
that still has
some fight left
after the world
tried to burn you
at the stake.
Now,
it beats
in flames.

CHRISTINA HART

PRAYING LIKE HELL

And all at once
there were all
these things
that needed to be done
and undone
and I didn't know
whether I should
put on my Sunday's best
and show up
at a church
I never went to
or pray like hell
that all this shit
would work itself out
on its own.

THERE IS BEAUTY IN THE BLEEDING

THE VOICES ARE NICE TODAY

I never said
I wanted the voices
to go away.
I just wish
they had nicer
things to say.

CHRISTINA HART

UNTITLED AND UNREALIZED

It must be so quiet
in a vacuum.
It must be so dull
at the edge of a knife.
At the bottom
of a purse,
it must be so lonely.
But at the tip of the world
as it spins and spins
it must be so peaceful.
I was never a ballerina
but just for one
everlasting moment
I'd like to be that
elegant centerpiece
of a little girl's musical
jewelry box, spinning
and spinning.
But it's not about
the dance,
it's about being someone
a little girl could look up to.
God, it's so quiet
in this vacuum.
But at least no one
can look down at me in here.

POTENTIAL, WE ALL HAVE IT

We carry potential
like dead weight.

CHRISTINA HART

I AM LIKE OTHER GIRLS

I hate when girls say
"I'm not like other girls"
because, aren't they?
I am. I'm like other girls.
Maybe louder than some,
softer than some,
harder than some.
But like them, I know
what sadness tastes like.
I, too, have the words
"I thought you were different"
stained on my lips
in different shades
for men who were
also just like other men,
the same man who
came and went
wearing many different faces.
I, too, know the power
that rests between
my bosom and my belly.
And just like other girls,
I have been conditioned
to say "sorry"
even when
I am not wrong.

THERE IS BEAUTY IN THE BLEEDING

I BUILD WALLS, TOO

Let's tear down
our walls
and then
build them
back up
by scratch,
together.

CHRISTINA HART

IF YOU ARE BAD

Good men will suffer
because of you and
the decent ones
will never stand a chance.
And one day, will you pay?
Will you finally pay for
all that you took from me?
For all the things you stole
from my future?
Will you pay for this heart
you broke
and then fixed not to trust?
Will you pay for the pain
you poured into my eyes?'
For the damage you
built into my bones?
For the good in me
you siphoned out?
Because one day,
you will.

THERE IS BEAUTY IN THE BLEEDING

I WILL EAT YOU

Sometimes people
leave me
with such a
bad taste
in my mouth
I swear
I'll never
eat again.

WHAT IF

Football field lights and
the last time you
asked me to dance.
I was wearing skin
I wasn't quite yet
comfortable in.
Your hands,
shaky and unsure.
Mine, fumbling somewhere
between your hair and
this is it. A first kiss.
Or not.
A first regret.
A "what if" that may
hold us hostage
for the rest of our lives.
A "what if" left off
at the precise moment
that if I ever see you again,
I will kiss you and
you will expect it this time.

TODAY IS FOR ME?

I lived
so many yesterdays
for you.
But today,
today is for me.

CHRISTINA HART

HE WAS EASY TO FALL IN LOVE WITH

He was easy to
fall in love with,
like a quiet snowfall
on a cold night
when you didn't realize
you were waiting
for something beautiful
to happen.

SOMETIMES IT'S JUST THAT SIMPLE

And just like that,
you came and made me
feel things
I thought
I'd never feel again.
Sometimes it's just
that simple.

IT'S A SICK GAME

I'm sorry I don't have
more words for you.
You haven't hurt me,
and this thing I feel—
I think they call it "happy"—
I am still processing it.
Because when I saw you
I was afraid my eyes
would turn into pearls.
I labeled you "danger"
and proceeded anyway.
I was sure you would
hurt me and I was sure
I would like it.
It's a sick game
I play with myself, I know.
I'm disturbed, I know.
Please excuse me if I don't know
what to do with you.
If I do not tell you
that I want to make a home
in your dimples.
If I do not say I'm not sorry
you haven't hurt me.

THERE IS BEAUTY IN THE BLEEDING

MAYBE WE'RE ALL PLAYING

Maybe we're all doomed.
Maybe none of us are.
But I'd like to think that
we'll all ride tricycles off
into the sunset
in the pouring rain
without being afraid
of getting a little wet.

WHAT IT MEANS

Without tragedy
we wouldn't learn
what it means to be
utterly and absolutely
human,
and maybe,
just maybe,
something even
a little bit more.

TO DESERVE BETTER

I can see the holes
in your eyes
where the hope used to be
and I can see the knot
in your throat
from every disappointment
you've had to swallow.
And I know,
I know you wonder
why it is so easy
for them to leave you.
And I wish I had an answer,
but I only have a reminder:
You deserved so much better.

CHRISTINA HART

THERE IS BEAUTY IN THE BLEEDING

CHRISTINA HART

THERE IS BEAUTY IN THE BLEEDING

Instagram: christinakaylenhart
Twitter: ChristinaKHart
Email: christinakaylenhart@gmail.com

Made in the USA
Lexington, KY
01 February 2018